Ulster Catharsis

A Cycle of Poems on Emigration, Breakdown, Return and Healing

by

Jeffrey Lamont

Bloomington, IN

authorHOUSE®

Milton Keynes, UK

AuthorHouse™
1663 Liberty Drive, Suite 200
Bloomington, IN 47403
www.authorhouse.com
Phone: 1-800-839-8640

AuthorHouse™ UK Ltd.
500 Avebury Boulevard
Central Milton Keynes, MK9 2BE
www.authorhouse.co.uk
Phone: 08001974150

First published by AuthorHouse 7/10/2006

ISBN: 1-4259-4138-9 (sc)

Printed in the United States of America
Bloomington, Indiana

This book is printed on acid-free paper.

Contents

INNOCENCE

Ode to a Man Telling Yarns*

(10th May 2005)

You'd see him toilin' in the soil
Pratie bags tied roun his knees,
In his little wee back garden
Hoein' spuds an' stakin peas.

But most times ye would find him
Wae his Grandwanes, on a dake,
Tellin' yarns an singin' songs
A rare oul' Ulster rake.

Aye, he would tell ye rare yins
O' the Scallys o' the moss,
An folks way doun in Novally
Miss Mary Ann and wee Dan Ross.

He toul this yin on Archie
Bout the wee man lukin Cavan,
Says Archie 'tell me when you're bulled'
An' I'll tell ye when you're cavin'.

Saturday nights down in McKeague's
He'd have his porter treats,
Then trudge back up to Knocklayde View
Wi his pockets full o' sweets.

The wanes they surely loved him
He was Santa come too soon,
An' he'd empty oot his pockets
An' they a would gether roun.

An' proud tae Craigalappin
On the twelfth day of July,
With his collar an' his bowler
An' the bunting flying high.

An' he'd tell ye o' the little folk,
Spied on McGowan's hill,
An' if I'm in Broughgammon
I swear I see them still.

Jamie Christie o' Broughgammon
Was everybody's friend,
But he was my Grandfather
And to him these thoughts I send.

* Memories of my maternal Grandfather, with whom, regretfully, I never resolved our politico-religious differences. Now I see the wisdom of all he said.

'Fort Apache' (Knocklayde View)*

5th June 2005

Bridget Winter was the first, the guardian of the hedge,
Sadie and Mrs Murdoch, I think they took the pledge.

Johnny and Sadie they came next, manicuring their wee lawn,
The Connors all once lived at four, like many they are gone.

Piggy raved at number five, his discos they were fine,
The McLernons still at number six, have been there a lifetime.

Dan Cunningham, the quiet man, still drives a steady pace,
And alas the poor McGarrys have stared murder in the face.

Of Katie's brood, so many, King Billy is left standing,
And the Hill sisters at number ten, kooking from the landing.

But the Kooking King must be Maquire, neck craned in rapt attention,
Kathleen Lamont, her garden fair, and Tommy in detention.

Big John, Big John, and Mrs Mac, the boss and the subverted,
While Ivy waits for Charlie's calls, we thought it quite perverted.

And the Carsons saw their share of grief, just like so many others,
Big Charlie swaying up the street, to slip beneath the covers.

The Connors, were they nine or ten?, it's very hard to say,
Big Eileen she penned 'Duncan' up, ne'er saw the light of day.

Pa Mooney with his car agleam, he hated our football,
I smashed a goal one evening into Steven Nicholls hall.

The Wilkinsons, the breakfast folk, I think from Amazonia,
And the Starrs o'er in the corner, surrounded by begonia.

And next in line the Cookies came, Sean, Liam and Marie,
Then Ted and Margaret, BIG YVONNE, and that f**k**g dog Whiskee.

Then Ted and Mrs Varlow, they really were aloof,
We used to knock their door with string, from our old coalshed roof.

We're up to number twenty six, McCurdys here do dwell,
Monopoly in their garden shed, hotels to buy and sell.

James McAfee he was no doubt the best friend of my Dad,
And then the 'window-climber', Graham, first bird he ever had.

And what to say of Aggie, with her verbose Minah bird?
And Geordie on the squeeze-box, the finest ever heard.

The Dunlops were at twenty nine, but both have passed away,
And Francis on his motorbike, that awful fateful day.

And we sorely do miss Heggarty, my God she was a gas,
Throwing Billy's worldly goods, from bedroom onto grass.

The McCaughans were a motley crew, Jack and Minnie in the van,
And poor Randal the demented, out in his wee bread van.

But just who lived at thirty three, is beyond me to say,
But Annie she's a stalwart, and she rounds off to this day.

Aye, we were all so happy, every neighbour was your friend,
And to their lasting memory, it's these few lines I've penned.

* Fond reminiscences of growing up in Knocklayde View, Ballycastle.

Townlands[1]

(June 2005)

'Ye can straddle four townlands right here',
Jamie Christie said to me,
On a Summer's day so long ago,
Beneath an old thorn tree.

Sitting in the sunshine,
And proud of his wee farm,
Wi his trousers tae his oxters[2],
Round me, a loving arm.

'One corner is Faltaggart,
And dear Broughgammon too,
On the East side lies oul' Isl-na-nagh[3],
Magherycastle by the bru'.

He puffed his pipe, he told a yarn,
He played a trick or two,
He was a poet in command,
Of all that was in view.

And now that I am older,
And I puff my pipe as well,
I often think wi' ae' fond smile,
Of the tales that he did tell.

Aye, the fairy folk were dancin',
In a corner of his land,
And a hare became a Goblin,
With a wave of his brown hand.

He'd take the snow and add some milk,
And ye would have ice-cream,
An' pocketfuls of liquorice sweets,
To spice our childhood dream.

His generation are all gone,
It is our greatest loss,
In the land o' dreams and fairies,
My Granda was the boss.

Notes for the non-Irish:-

1. A townland is the smallest administrative sub-division of land in Ireland. There are some 80,000 townlands in Ireland.

2. Oxters = armpits. My Granda, like most of his generation, would wear his trousers very high, with the waistband approaching his oxters.

3. Isl-na-nagh is the name of a townland beside my Granda's farm, meaning, in old Irish, 'the island of horses'.

Tramp (On a walk from Ballycastle to the Lag Tower[1])

Tramp the County Antrim, boys
Tramp her up an doun
Tramp her frae the Port West Strand
Tae the Lammas, Dullas[2], toun

Tramp her tae the Lag round tower
By the village aff the plain[3]
Tramp her sheughs[4] and ditches
That I played in as a wane[5]

Tramp her by the limeworks
Where me Mother used to toil[6]
An on doun tae Dunseverick
By the fiesty Sea of Moyle

Aye, tramp the cliffs and seashores
Where aft times I hae been
With the vista oot tae Rachery[7] isle
The fairest ever seen

And on and on tae Slemish
As Holy as ye can[8]
And thank the Lord that you were born
A County Antrim man.

Notes:-

1. The Lag Tower is a 7th Century Round Tower near Armoy, used by the clerics at the nearby church to escape the wrath of invading Vikings.

2. The Lammas, Dullas toun refers to Ballycastle, specifically the famous Lammas Fair and the great edible seaweed sold there, 'Dulce', locally called Dullas.

3. 'The Village Aff the Plain' refers to the village of Armoy, which, translated from original Irish, means The Village Off the Plain.

4. For the non-Irish, a sheugh is a watery ditch.

5. 'Wane' is Ulster and West Scottish for child.

6. As a young woman, my Mother worked in Capecastle Limeworks, on the slopes of Knocklayde Mountain.

7. 'Rachery' is the local name for Rathlin Island.

8. Slemish Mountain, near Ballymena, is a holy site because it was here that Saint Patrick, as a young man, was held captive as a swine-herd after being kidnapped in Wales.

The 'Christian' Bum Boy*

December 2005

With the 'Christians' to Glengonnar,
T'was to be a holy jaunt,
Little knowing pious Lindsey,
Would our innocence affront.

Clutching Bibles to Glengonnar,
Mister Brown seemed heaven-sent,
A sleep-over for bad behaviour,
Now we know just what it meant.

Bible readings, 'finding' Jesus,
C.S.S.M. Bar B Q's,
With ten-year-olds, young eyes a-goggle,
Lindsey knew he couldn't lose.

They made it clear we were unholy,
Lindsey a Christian paragon,
But now the truth is out in public,
His clerical cover it is gone.

Years before in Ballycastle,
Guitars and Gospel on the strand,
Lindsey started grooming early,
Feely-touchy happy band.

And yet he's not the only one,
In grammar schools and church recesses,
With left hand deftly cassocks lifting,
While right the victim children blesses.

So when I see the 'pillars',
Of this hypocrite society,
I am a cynic and a sceptic,
Because I've seen it all, you see.

* My early exposure to the holy Christians, and a very narrow escape!

Me Granny

January 2006

Me Granny died at 93,
As sprightly as a trout,
No cancer, no pneumonia,
Not even any gout.

To her the God 'gymnasium',
A deity quite remote,
An' ye should have seen the feedin'
That she put down her throat.

Milk that wasn't pasteurised,
Fried soda and fried fadge,
And eggs and loads o' bacon,
'Eating healthy' not her badge.

And swimmin', that was somethin'
Sticklebacks did in the burn,
Grown folks in bathing costumes,
Would surely make her turn.

And jogging the Queen's highway,
That would rightly bring her frowns,
Although she rode her bicycle,
High saddled up to Browns.

So as you eat your rabbit food,
Nibble lettuce and gym sweat,
Reflect that not a single one of you,
Has outlived me Granny yet........

Nor will ye, for me Granny
Was of a hardy breed,
No slave to fad and fashion,
Nor stressed out by lust and greed.

She was a daughter of the soil,
Simple, pure, replete,
The finest, kindest woman,
That I've ever chanced to meet.

No credit cards nor bank accounts,
Her cash stashed by the bed,
And her dear old family bible,
Cherished and well read.

She's gone but not forgotten,
And her lessons still abide,
Be good, do good to fellow man,
And shun those full of pride.

The Trampit Hen*

February 2006

The trampin' o' a turkey hen's
A serious affair,
And here's a tale o' a poor oul' hen,
Was trampit wi' great flair.

Me Great Granny says to Granda,
Now take this fine she-beast,
And march her oot tae Scallys',
And tramp her yince at least.

So underneath the oxter
Of the puzzled little boy,
Went the great expectant turkey,
Like a much-prized Christmas toy.

But the roddin tae Scallys' loanin,
It was long and hot and dry,
And me Granda wasney willin',
However he might try.

Says he tae himsel', this trampin
So hard it cannae be,
So he tied the hen's oul' gobbly neck,
To a wee sapling Ash tree.

With jacket off and shirt sleeves rolled,
And hob-nails flying fast,
He tramped and tramped and further tramped,
Till the beast expired at last.

Now, satisfied and sweating,
His quarry dead in tow,
He sauntered back along the lane,
Tae Great Granny he did go.

'Lord blissis, son, what hae' ye done,
She's me pride and joy that hen,
An' when I want the next yin tramped,
I'll naw send ye again'.

So the moral of this turkey's death,
Is plain for all to see,
When ye need tae have a turkey tramped,
Don't send a boy of three!!

* A story told about my maternal Great Granny and Granda. Poor turkey!

INNOCENCE LOST

Rage*

December 1999

Oh, how many times,
In how many places,
Have I lain down?
On oil-stained sheets,
Stiff expectancy being purged,
To quell the pressing rage.

Unwanted, pleasurable fury,
Burning in my soul,
Burning through my soul,
To bring but illusory joy,
And one step closer to losing,
Losing all I love.

* Mania brings with it its own brand of hedonistic libido, untameable, and ultimately totally destructive.

Ismailova* Reprise

(June 2005)

In Russia they're so friendly,
When it suits them so to be,
Especially when they want to get
Something from you and me.

But society is ugly,
And the manners still are grim,
And I never did get to interview
The great 'Legenda Krim'.

The men they are so macho,
Every woman like a whore,
Oh, Ismailova Metro
I don't want to see you more.

Nepotistic sychophants,
Grovelling to 'the boss',
Huddled, sweating cattle
As the Metro lines they cross.

'Thank you' or 'please' escapes them,
As they look from blank, dead eyes,
If one in a million is polite,
My God, what a surprise!

Security, they love it,
With gorillas at each door,
This season 'knee-length' shorts are 'in',
Swaggering on the floor.

Glasnost and Perestroika,
Have not quite perculated,
And a Russian civic society
Is a concept quite belated.

And beaurocracy, they love it,
So many forms to fill,
And if rudeness was as sharp as steel,
Receptionists could kill.

Mobile phones, gold jewellery,
At every twist and turn,
The 'Nove Russki' they are thriving,
But still so taciturn

The so-called music is so loud,
The neon lights are bright,
And all across this city
The Mafia rule the night.

I have been here for one week,
Seems such a long, long time,
In this soviet-cowboy country,
Thank God it isn't mine!

* Ismailova is an out-lying district of Moscow, last visited by the author in 1998. Upon staying there again in June 2005, he was not completely surprised to see no evidence of changes to the brutish, swaggering, rude, and psychologically constipated nature of Russian society.

Bashkiriya

(July 2005)

She was working in Saint Petersburg,
Dealing in heady time,
And she counted every dollar,
And she took my every dime.

But I walked the path of ill-repute,
With my lady of the night,
Taking head on unmade beds,
Self-control way out of sight.

She was sexy and capricious,
As such girls they usually are,
And we lived on Nevsky Prospekt,
Every restaurant and bar.

Manic and depressive,
I lived my double life,
Nearly gave up my dear children,
And I sacrificed my wife.

And when at last the race was run,
When lust had turned to hate,
I tried to lead a normal life,
Alas, it was too late.

What goes around sure comes around,
Destruction's seeds were sown,
I tasted bitter-sweetness,
Like I have never known.

So young men, when you travel,
And the girls will sport and play,
Remember those who love you,
Do not throw your life away.

* An unfortunate encounter with the seedy underworld of Saint Petersburg, Russia.

Natasha*

December 1999

Cold on Tverskaya,
I took her mute off the street.
Building passion on paper
Over beers in La Cantina.

We queued for cash,
And when we got home,
We devoured each other,
I heard her first, and last, utterance.

Was she really a Svetlana?

* Aliterally Mute Moscow Madness.

Bad Libido*

(June 2005)

Inappropriate behaviour,
Of the naughty, sexual kind,
Can happen any time or place,
When you have lost your mind.

May be on an escalator,
Or it may be in a lift,
But such anti-social urges,
Are so difficult to shift.

When your eyes are busy looking,
But your hands were made to touch,
It's hard to put the brakes on,
When you get that heady rush.

It can grab you in a nightclub,
Or hi-jack you in a train,
But boy, the morning after,
It can cause you so much pain.

It could happen out in Moscow,
Or at home here in Coleraine,
But from such erotic pleasures,
It is so hard to refrain.

But now I take my Lithium,
Sedated night and day,
So I don't get no more urges,
Bad Libido's gone away!

Hurray!

* I owe my relative sanity to Doctor Bell.

Manic With McMahon

(November 2002)

When we cried together,
We didn't know that we were twins,
A pair.
Weeping in Manhattan,
In MD despair.

We travelled far, we travelled wide,
One thing you never took, I lost,
To MD,
A bride.

And so, like all,
We touched as ships,
Upon the MD night,
Where'ere you are, I wish,
That you're alright.

On Tverskaya

December 1999

On such an infamous Ulitsa.
I should run again,
Driven.
From what, I know not,
To what, I have known many times.
Unrealised expectancy, shame,
A poorer, madder man.

Dubious Friend

January 2006

A dubious friend came slinking
By my house the other night,
He clawed my doors and windows,
And he gave me such a fright.

For I thought we'd parted company,
Long said our last farewell,
But he was on my threshold,
Intent on merry hell.

But I am weak, polite you know,
So I drew him to the fire,
We planned our usual exploits,
And the omens they were dire.

For by the glowing embers,
He cast his Faustian spell,
I knew where I was going,
As into his arms I fell.

Down down into the wicked dream,
My mind and soul distorted,
As through his many mansions,
We danced and we cavorted.

At daybreak I awoke, quite dazed,
My friend he had departed,
And I was left with ashes gray,
Something new, yet old, imparted.

He was no friend, has never been,
Since Adam and the fall,
Beware, my friend, the very dubious
Friend called alcohol.

Icarus

March 2006

Bred a deep, deep tumbler,
He fell, precipitous,
In the world of high high flyers,
Alas it's often thus.

For he spread his wings unto the stars,
Like Icarus the sun,
To Jupiter and Venus,
Until he was undone.

For flying's not for feeble hearts,
Nor yet for feeble minds,
For storms are there a blowing,
Demons of many kinds.

And yet he flew for many,
To them he brought great hope,
But the fatal flaw was lurking,
With the height he could not cope.

So now he's fluttered to the Earth,
His feet have turned to clay,
Outwatered in North Antrim,
Where he spends the fitful day.

BREAKDOWN

Run For Home/The Girl
From Taldysuu

(June 2005)

Cycling fast in '98,
In Moscow, mania, reeling,
Now I'm on the Belfast boat,
Devoid of any feeling.

Too many moons in exile,
No comfort zones for me,
Till at last, beyond the bow,
It's Ulster's shores I see.

My Mother, firm foundation,
Is waiting on the shore,
Oh, at times I really thought,
I ne'er would see her more.

Diagnosis, medication,
The tears in rivers flow,
I never would have tramped so far,
If I'd known what I now know.

Denial, and acceptance,
Follow on each others heels,
Still no one really understands,
Just how this MD feels.

In bars for consolation,
With alcohol, 'my friend',
Drinking, stumbling, mumbling,
In the hope that it will end.

And then, like light from Heaven,
Way out in Kyrgyzstan,
I met the girl from Taldysuu,
Who made me a whole man.

It is Aigul from Taldysuu,
To whom I owe my life,
Whom I will love and cherish,
And whom I'll make my wife.

Two Years

(January 1999)

I've always had two years to go,
And then I'd have a life,
But all I've done is lose my mind,
My kids, my house, my wife.

In just two years I'd have a home,
Somewhere I could live,
But now I know the price to pay,
Was much too much to give.

I knew two years would soon go bye,
I'd be a normal bloke,
But now I know that dreams like these,
Are just a sorry joke.

I've waited and I've waited,
For my two years to fly,
But two years have become full ten,
And still I sit and cry.

In just two years I'd make a stash,
Mercedes in the drive,
But now I'm lost, I just don't know,
For what it is I strive.

Yes, two years, ten, of waiting,
I've had a life of pain,
Twenty four months of waiting,
Can drive you mad, insane.

And so I sit here homeless,
Friendless and alone,
During two years, ten, of waiting,
Just what have I done?

By Mutual Agreement

January 2000

Tallahaugh, the low place of that burn,
For which I broke my heart and bent my mind,
My house, but never quite my home.
Housing happily my wife and children,
Whilst I wander,
Occasionally to inhabit the music room,
By mutual agreement.

The Borders, dull land of overwhelming hills,
In which I honed my moods and learned to shy,
A home to many, but never fully mine.
Accents of Burns and Scott, and Hogg,
Whilst I secretly prayed to Heaney, Hewitt and Morrison,
True home denied,
By mutual agreement.

Then Mother Russia, never to be understood in the mind,
The best of homes, and the worst too,
Killing with delight.
Expansive, grandiose, and cold,
She took me to her bosom,
I grew there some new roots,
By mutual agreement.

And back to Ulster, cradle of my youth,
Province of blood, so precious,
So many have for her died.
Renewing a sense of belonging,
A sense of self, long lost,
Blending to rock and wave,
In fusion so sublime,
By mutual agreement.

LOSS

Ours

(February 2000)

Ours was the giant, on our beloved strand,
Where first we wandered, hand in hand,
Ours was the wind and the Atlantic foam,
When first to Ireland you did roam.

Ours was Rathlin, our sceptered isle,
The red Irish Fuschia and the Camomile,
Ours was Fairhead, walks in the rain,
Long long before we knew of pain.

Ours was your room in Manor House,
Where we stole quiet as a mouse,
Ours was to make there love so fine,
Those early days, when you were mine.

Ours tramping roads and hitching lifts,
Your smile and laughs such wondrous gifts,
Ours touching feet in sweet Portrush,
When I learned to love you oh so much.

Ours McCarrolls pub, Bodhran thumping loud,
When we spied each other from the crowd,
Ours hot halfs and porter fine,
When at last I met a mind for mine.

Ours the three children who eventually came,
To mention all three by name,
Patrick, Dominik and sweet Anna too,
A lasting sign of my love for you.

Ours alas was the fate of many's a pair,
Of life's ups and downs we had our share,
My illness worsened down the years,
Now I'm alone and full of tears.

And so I know I'll never find,
So sweet a one, so true and kind,
Who picked me up and helped me grow,
The sweetest love I'll ever know.

Lay Down

(March 2000)

Well I lay down with many
And liked but a few.
Only once have I loved
And that was with you.

I seemed to be bad
When I was really but mad.
But it had the effect
That our love it has wrecked.

So when you are weary
And in need of a rest,
Lay down and think fondly
Of the man you loved best.

A tragedy o'er took him
In the prime of his life,
When he lost his children
And he lost you, his wife.

And think you some more
On the death of his will,
For you deserted and left him
When he was lonely and ill.

Aye think ye a bit
On what he's had to come to,
And pray God that it never
Ever happens to you.

Fairweather ~~Friends~~ Fascists

(July 2005)

Dear Liberal Fascists, you know who,
Here's a ditty just for you,
Fairweather friends, who are withal,
Not really friends at all.

As Irish comic, I was wanted,
But now with truth I have affronted,
Christian values hypocritic,
As 'Homophobe', I'm parasitic.

Glen No (Popularly known as Glencoe)

December 2005

To a tiny, bitter, snowy glen,
Way up into the North,
A bloody band of Campbells
Sallied forth.

Aye they went to earn their shilling,
In the payment of the Crown,
And they sned a few MacDonalds,
Cut them down.

Nor it wasney very many,
That they bled there in the snow,
But the spin of several centuries,
Won't let go.

While down upon the Cowal,
Not many of you know,
Proud Lamont's fate was sealed,
By that same foe.

Great Lamont of all Cowal,
Put his hand tae Campbell's writ,
An' the Campbells threw it over,
Cruel wit.

Wi' sword an' torch they pillaged,
Round ancient Ascog and Dunoon,
An' the lovely Toward Castle,
Tumbled doon.

O'er twa hundred special gentlemen,
O' the Lamonts they were flung,
Into the Toward graveyard,
And then hung.

An' the lecherous brute Campbells,
They raped oor lassies fair,
An' frae that day our great clan,
Was nae mair.

But the 'massacre' that's always,
On the tip of every tongue,
Is Glencoe, MacDonalds woes
Well sung.

Yet Lamonts in their thousands,
Fled Argylshire up and down,
And assumed the names of White,
And Black and Brown.

So if you're in the midgelands,
And true massacre will see,
Take yersel' tae Dunoon,
By the sea.

And gaze upon a monument,
Just aff the braw sea-front,
Tae 1642 and the finish
Of Lamont.

The Parish, and the Damage Done

January 2006

To pluck the boy from parish,
And his backward, simple mind,
But a question of Geography,
While transport he can find.

But to pluck those learned behaviours,
From his later, fever'd brain,
Is something his psychiatrist,
All his skill upon must train.

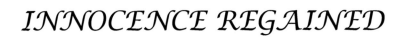

INNOCENCE REGAINED

Exiles

(*June 2005*)

Samuel Beckett said 'I'm out of here',
James Joyce he said 'me too',
'A Terrible Beauty has been born',
A scourge to me and you'.

George Bernard Shaw hit London town,
And Oscar he came too,
To join the other exiles,
A million? One or two.

And Van the Man he sailed away,
From war-torn Belfast town,
James Galway he soon followed suit,
And looked back with a frown.

From sport, George Best has left us,
Hurricane Higgins too,
To find more peaceful, liberal shores,
To start their life anew.

Sure, 15 US Presidents,
From Ulster they did sail,
Across the wild Atlantic,
While their kin did weep and wail.

But Yeats he lingered, so forlorn,
In his barren Sligo seat,
To muse upon his long-lost love,
With clay upon her feet.

But I am happy in this land,
From which our Clan sprang forth,
An exile I'll no longer be,
To East, South, West or North.

Vive la Revolution!

(June 2005)

I think I am a Socialist,
A le grande idée Francais,
Throughout my life I've practiced,
A true Egalite.

Prime Ministers or cleaners,
I have known them all by name,
Religion, race or status,
I just treat them all the same.

Yes, I must be a Socialist,
Fraternity, not fame,
My friends in every Continent,
I love them all the same.

For Liberte I've done my share,
Poor peoples I've assisted,
It's strange that all my life, the title,
'Socialist' I've resisted.

Black Dog

October 2005

Churchill had his Black Dog,
So often in his lair,
Van he had his moody blues,
To wail out his despair.

Spike he had his humour,
And he had us all in tears,
While Vincent painted fury,
To quell the manic fears.

Yes, everyone his own way,
To cope with cruel MD,
Medication and my woman,
And no alcohol for me.

For I've walked Churchill's Black Dog,
And I've sung Van's blackest blues,
My poetry like paintings,
Echoes Vincent's inner muse.

Wrens

March 2006

At Benvarden, in the Jasmine tree,
There flit two spatting Wrens,
Perchance, two Springtime lovers,
Or yet, not even friends.

For friends have walked as lovers,
On some romantic shore,
But flitting and a spatting,
Lovers they're no more.

But Spring it is a good time,
To think and make amends,
No more to be as lovers,
But at least to talk as friends.

For time and tide it changes us,
And makes us wise with age,
To quell hate and suspicion,
And to take away the rage.

So raise a cup in every airt,
To those who would be friends,
Not to spat and fret and worry,
Like Benvarden's Springtime Wrens.

*STILL ANGRY AFTER
ALL THESE YEARS*

ROOM 101

(June 2005)

Forty-five and angry,
Whatever can it be?
In this glorious PC world of ours,
With reality TV.

I'm a homophobe, a racist,
A sexist, so you see,
I've always been a misfit,
That's what's really wrong with me.

A misfit who loathes football,
And sport of any kind,
Who'd rather not have brawn at all,
But rather have a mind.

I am not pierced nor tattooed,
I do not read the Sun,
But 80% of people do,
Sometimes I want to run!

Celebrities I cannot stand,
Nothing to celebrate,
If I see no more make-overs,
Would already be too late.

If Posh and Becks would drop down dead,
I'd surely jump for joy,
Imagine giving such a name,
To their poor bastard little boy.

And Geldof and Sir Bono,
What bloody hypocrites,
To paraphrase John McEnroe,
'You really are the pits'.

And glamour sluts and macho men,
Paraded on TV,
But who they are, or what they do,
Is a mystery to me.

From BBC, the opium,
Capricious and mind-numbing,
At six o'clock the anchor girls,
The Establishment's view summing.

And at the centre, Labour,
Behind Blair's gleaming grin,
Their promises to one and all,
Are wearing mighty thin.

Cult*

The cult of personality,
Perverse and sick, it seems to me,
Nepotistic Psychophancy,
Psychological infancy.

For the 'big' man the people clamour,
But fail to see behind the glamour,
Yet I've seen many 'off the stage',
Hypocricy fills me with rage.

For no matter how they rant and rail,
Like you and me they are but frail,
And spin their image as they may,
They are but men, with feet of clay.

Humility, modesty, I say,
Rare virtues in this present day,
The 'biggest' man, you know he must,
Shuffle off, return to dust.

For me, myself, I've always striven,
Not by my ego to be driven,
Although I have achieved much more,
Than any 'powerful' railing bore.

Excellent degrees I have a few,
I've researched, lectured, published too,
And languages I learn for fun,
But the limelight? – that I shun.

For what's a man with puff and bluster,
Who cannot true compassion muster,
His giant ego so inflated,
In his last years, regrets belated.

* This poem was written in the foyer of the Ismailova Hotel, Moscow, after the author was treated to a 2-hour long, self-aggrandising, speech by an 'important' man, like so many hundreds the author has listened to before. The 'important' man was full of himself, but actually so full of shit!

On the Outside

(June 2005)

Always on the outside,
Never managed to get in,
Singing my own rebel song,
Midst life's incessant din.

I can't understand football,
Nor sport of any kind,
It has to be cerebral,
Living in my mind.

Those people who chase money,
Coveting with greed,
I never could quite understand,
What is it that they need?

And those who crave the peaks of power,
Destroying as they go,
The lives that they have blighted,
Will they ever really know?

I'll sit and write my poems a while,
And puff the odd cigar,
I'm happier than the richest man,
Or most powerful, oh by far.

I've sailed earth's seven oceans,
To her four corners I have been,
And nought but greed and avarice,
In every place I've seen.

So money make the world go round,
And people take your share,
But I'm happier here in Antrim,
Than to clamour way out there.

Joy of Credit

January 2006

I need that Shreiber kitchen,
It'll be my peace of mind,
Then I can really hob-nob,
With Acacia Avenue in kind.

We've candles in the bathroom,
Every room without a book,
And we're shopping in Ikea,
For that continental look.

The kids are in X-factor,
Auditioning for the show,
Trained on pub Karaoke,
They'll win it, don't you know.

And we want a Spanish villa,
For those long weekends away,
Or a farmhouse renovation,
In the depths of Normandy.

I've just got my 13th credit card,
With APR 13,
And a cash-back convertible option,
Whatever does it mean?

And the Lexus is just wonderful,
The Jones' heads do turn,
This retail therapy's just the thing,
With credit cards to burn.

And Aaron's into grammar school,
He'll have an old school tie,
And goodness knows what privilege,
It eventually will buy.

And I love our new Jacuzzi,
With the decking out the back,
And the recycled, organic furniture,
It really is the crack.

We've TVs now in every room,
But they're only 40 inch,
So with my brand new credit card,
We'll upgrade, it's a cinch!

And we do our bit for charity,
Orphans, donkeys get their share,
And to that great Bob Geldof,
For debt-relief somewhere.

We're in the gym ten times a week,
The sunbeds are included,
I'm looking in the mirror now,
Pure fitness, class exuded.

My husband doesn't mind the cost,
I'm worth it all you see,
I just wish sometimes he was at home,
To sit and talk with me.

He's always at the golfclub,
Or in the pub with friends,
On Saturday the football,
I wish he'd make amends.

And I think Alicia's pregnant,
Every morning she is ill,
But she never does confide in me,
Perhaps one day she will.

So you see I am the woman,
Who has everything she needs,
So why do I cry myself to sleep,
My soul, in credit, bleeds.

THOUGHTS FROM THE SMOKING ROOM

The Time of Her Life

(July 2005)

'Menopausal Madness',
That's what the 'experts' said,
God only knows what's going on,
Inside that woman's head.

Hysteria, Depression,
Follow on each other's heels,
Me, I'm Manic Depressive,
So I know just how she feels.

She loves him, and she hates him,
Her world in carrier bags,
Terror for the children,
While her skin it droops and sags.

Midnight dash to freedom,
Down to her childhood lair,
To torture Kate and Tommy,
It really isn't fair.

Whiskey for survival,
And bed ten times a day,
Like a willow in the wind,
Resolve does bend and sway.

How much longer can she teeter,
On this infernal brink?
I fear the crunch is coming,
And it's time to swim – or sink!

In the Lion's Den

(*June 2005*)

They claim to follow Abraham
And Moses, that great Jew,
But they desecrate the Jewish faith,
And the holy Torah too.

Of the Mishnah and Gemarrah,
Their ignorance is replete,
But they scrape and bow to a Jewish boy,
They weep at Jesus' feet.

They've reinvented Shabbat,
When they pray and sing their song,
Dismissing those who Sinai's
Cruel desert knew so long.

The Holy book, 'their' Bible,
It is bound in blood and skin,
But do they know which wilderness is
Gathering all her children in?

And I've seen them fighting Buddha,
And the Hindu children too,
Their damned churches in Cambodia,
A sacrilege to view.

And they'll preach to you from Romans,
That the Jews should acquiesce,
According to that fascist saint,
Who created such a mess.

The Dusky Maiden

(August 2005)

Among life's little pleasures,
The best for me, by far,
Retiring to my smoking room,
To puff a good cigar.

But only fine Havanas,
Cohiba, Partagas, or Punch,
In the stillness of the morning,
Or after a good lunch.

Rolled on a dusky maiden's thigh,
In dear old Fidel's land,
With filler, binder, wrapper,
And topped with a golden band.

Puffing on my Puros,
My fermented, hand-made friend,
It's manys a poem or ditty,
In the smoking room I've penned.

They say that they will kill me,
And maybe that is true,
But cancer-riddled abstainers,
I've also seen a few.

To Benvarden from Gibraltar,
The Customs circumvent,
So manys a happy hour,
In the smoking room I've spent.

Mark Twain recounts the pleasure,
'Midst the cares that hedge the day',
To light a good Havana,
And to 'puff life's cares away'.

So like Mark Twain I'm puffing,
As life's cares they pass me bye,
Thinking of old Castro,
And that dusky maiden's thigh.

Fault Line*

(August 2005)

My home town of Ballycastle,
Like a Bosnian fault line,
To the West a' my ain kith an' kin,
Tae the East they erny mine.

Ooot West o' Dunaninee,
Ulster Protestants abound,
Wi' their whitewashed farms and steadings,
And neat order all around.

While East frae Bonamargy,
Way up into the hills,
Dwell our Catholic Irish neighbours,
Brooding on historic ills.

East and West they co-exist,
In pubs and even churches,
But with politics so polarised,
Tragedy to crisis lurches.

But if you only scratch the surface,
Of these good Catholics and Prods,
You'll find suspicion, hatred,
That would invoke the gods.

So when you step out on Castle Street,
Why, never do forget,
It's Catholics and Prods you meet,
And not a person yet.

* The author has worked extensively in the Balkans, where the ethnic fault lines are so perceptibly raw. He sees his own home town, Ballycastle in County Antrim, as a metaphorical fault line, with the native Irish in the Eastern hills, and the Planter on the Western plain. Co-existence of the two tribes during the current 'peace process' is deceptive. Scratch the surface of Irish or Planter and you will find enough hatred to rival Muslims and Serbs.

Van the Man

(July 2005)

Rev me up, Van the Man,
Rev me up, Rev me up,
Bright side of the road,
And that old be-bop-de-lup.

Mellow me, Mr Morrison,
Mellow me, Mellow me,
From the mystic wet garden,
To Coney in the sea.

Satisfy, Belfast boy,
Satisfy, Satisfy,
No longer need to ask,
The reason why.

Returning, Icon of an age,
Returning, Returning by the sea,
To the Ulster shore,
You and me.

On a Golden Autumn Day, Ivan George,
On a Golden Autumn Ulster Day,
That sweet refrain just takes,
Just takes my breath away.

Midas touch, our Ulster Rover,
Midas touch, Midas touch,
To whom we owe,
To whom we owe so much.

The Rotten Livers*

September 2005

The rotten-livers, men-a-plenty,
Throng the morn, and all time,
In the dingy diamond den.

Cold welcome for non-dealers,
Non-partakers,
Or those of other class or creed.

The limpin' hirplin' hippy,
On the day-shift, so laid-back,
Scores, and cracks another snort of crack.

Snippets of that beautiful (?!) game,
Or limpid gambles talked,
Poor fodder for the native in-blow.

The putrid-livers, some despondent,
Some aggressive, some don't know,
Supping incessant to glorious oblivion.

Past the witching hour, past sanity,
Fetid livers take the toll,
Till homeward, literally, they roll.

God-given morn, yet paranoid,
And shaking to their core,
Stumble to the dingy hole for more, more, more.

Time-bomb livers, but shells of men,
Devoid of purpose any,
Desperation and depression, I'll bet my every penny.

* Reflections on an Irish drinking den, and its patrons, much frequented during
mania, but never once enjoyed.

Skopske Merak (Northern Ireland version)

December 2005

I've stayed in Skopske Merak,
And for sure I'm coming back,
Because, outside of Belfast,
It surely is the crack.

For Spiro has his finger,
On every single guest,
And for serving up the Skopske beer,
Miki is the best.

And when I come into the bar,
When the EC's work is done,
I can speak German and Russian,
I feel I'm the only one.

And Zlatko entertains me,
With multi-lingual repartee,
And the language that we speak,
Is between him and me.

And when the working day is done,
And all I want is rest,
For comfort and the BBC,
The Merak is the best.

So listen all you tourists,
Who meander down this way,
If you book in for a weekend,
For ever you will stay.

The Sheraton and Hilton,
They really charge too much,
And what they're really missing,
Is the friendly, personal, touch.

Skopje, Macedonia, Skopske Merak Hotel, a big thank you.

POLITICAL DIVERSIONS

Brothers

(_July 2005_)

Two brothers who have seldom met,
Our Billy and Yehuda,
One from Ulster's Emerald shores,
And one from barren Judah.

Their States were born last Century,
Ethnic, religious havens,
Refuge from Jihad and IRA,
The circling terrorist ravens.

Through siege and slaughter, propaganda,
We have both stood fast,
The Jewish and the Calvinist,
We know the worst's not passed.

The liberal fascists hate us,
We do not suit their scheme,
In Tel-a-Viv and Belfast,
We don't have room to dream.

So, Billy and Yehuda,
Understand that you're soul-mates,
In Jerusalem and Belfast,
Victory comes to he who waits.

9-11*

(July 2005)

'I'm Irish too', the Yankee beamed,
As he grinned and shook my hand,
'And I know in poor old Ireland,
Proddy Brits have all the land'.

'So I'm glad I send some money,
To buy Semtex and arms,
So we will drive those Proddy Brits,
Off our ancestral farms'.

Says I, 'Who'll drive you Yankees,
Off the Indians' holy land?',
Hypocritic 'Irish-Americans',
Their crap I cannot stand.

For guns and bombs are very well,
To send Brits to Hell or Heaven,
But how they whinged, and how they cried,
Still do, post nine-eleven.

'Irish-American' policemen,
Paddy firemen as well,
One day donating money,
The next one, blown to Hell.

Yankee, put your house in order,
From hypocricy refrain,
And stay away from Ulster,
Where you've funded grief and pain.

* Memories of a bar in New York city, watching the so-called Irish-American patrons, mostly firemen and policemen, heroes of the city, putting their blood money into Bobby Sands-IRA collection boxes. And the barman telling me how Protestants were all evil bastards, legitimate targets in the holy war. Then came 9-11!!

The Experiment*

(September 2005)

As maggots suck the carcass dry,
So Tavaritch did the State,
And Gorbachev he stemmed the tide,
But too quickly, and too late.

Sovkhoz and Kolkhoz workers,
Did steal and cheat, and plunder,
Midst piles of vodka bottles strewn,
They ripped the dream asunder.

Locked in with lies of paradise,
And the rabid Western hordes,
At last the evil bent its knee,
And made plough-shares, not swords.

And still the years have come and gone,
Cowboy-capitalists hold sway,
For Tavaritch, crumbling concrete,
Rusted angle-iron every way.

So for what the millions sacrificed?
Good Kulaks led away?
For the dreams of Marx and Engels,
Two fantasising old Hevrai.

But the lasting damage, worst of all,
Is in the realm of mind,
Indifference and suspicion rife,
Especially to their own kind.

Such a land of vast potential,
But the people truly lost,
A socialist-communist experiment,
At such an awful cost.

So when you pampered Westerners,
Upon thoughts of socialism dwell,
Thank God you've never had to live,
In this mind-numbing hell.

* Having lived and worked for fourteen years midst the desperate, mind-altering tragedy that is the Former Soviet Union, I am angered every time I return to the UK to hear those living in the lap of capitalist democracy and luxury, complaining about the very capitalism which gives them freedom, and extolling the virtues of 'socialism'. They should come with me next time I am in Russia, and try 'heaven' for a while.

Bogey Men (aka Bogus Men)

September 2005

Starched collars, ties, designer-groomed,
Come hirplin' from the hill,
Green softly-softly Bogey men,
With instinct still to kill.

False etiquette and mealy-mouth,
Fool Albion she has swallowed,
But we have watched, while, cock-a-hoop,
In concessions they have wallowed.

But Ulster folk we are no fools,
We dismiss the collars, ties,
We see the age-old enemy,
Deftly spinning retro-lies.

And we are asked to govern,
With these killers, ne'er a frown,
To govern our wee Ulster,
With those who'd pull her down.

The might of Israel we have not,
She deals with terror too,
But we'll defend, last drop of blood,
From Bogey men like you.

In stammered Irish, laughable,
Your propaganda flows,
To protect Colombia's murderers,
Guilty, Ahern he knows.

And Adams, biggest laugh of all,
His Irish is a joke,
Should we believe it was the tongue,
His English ancestors spoke?

So, treat with Blair, and with Ahern,
Concessions come piecemeal,
But when at last the talking's stopped,
With us you'll have to deal.

For we've been here four hundred years,
Twice four hundred and more we'll be,
And still your callous terror,
Will not drive us to the sea.

Black Pig's Dyke

October 2005

Hadrian had his wall, we know,
Renowned from East to West,
To foil P-Celtic woad-dubbed hordes,
Who really were a pest.

And Offa's Dyke, a monument
Of Welsh Q-Celts' disdain,
Did hem them to the higher hills,
Away from Albion's plain.

Our Cruithin too, not so well known,
But Celtic just the same,
Built Black Pig's Dyke in borderlands,
To stem the men of Slane.

And to this day, we Cruithin kin,
Through terror, blood and tears,
Must bolster up our Black Pig's Dyke,
To quell our ancient fears.

For o'er that dyke they've come and gone,
So murd'rous in the night,
Our Yeomen, wives and children,
In cowardly terror down to smite.

Black Nebs

December 2005

By midden bred,
On Brochan fed,
Aye, Blacknebs every yin,
Our meetin' hoose the dankest ditch,
Oor treatment sic a sin.

We wrought this land,
Wi' blistered hand,
The linen an' shipbuildin',
Frae watery bog we made our mark,
Londonderry o'er tae Hilden.

The Penal times,
The death bell chimes,
We suffered o'er oor share,
In wooden boats Atlantic braved,
Presidential over there.

Freedom at stake,
Both sides the lake,
We rallied to the call,
Great Britannias bloody nose,
Frae Blacknebs one an' all.

Yet time and toil,
In blood-soaked soil,
Our nature has perverted,
Profiled now as reactionaries,
The Blacknebs are deserted.

Wi' ne'er a friend,
How will it end,
For Blacknebs, valiant, true,
Who feared not Kings nor no man,
For Ulster saw it through.

Go West Lamont

December 2005/January 2006

Sixteen fifty two bein' the date of the year,
And Campbell, so ruthless, the Cowal did clear,
The Lamonts, those still livin', bereft of the sod,
Took on their disguises, and prayed to their God.

And God he did answer, for forty before,
A settlement was begun on Ulster's sweet shore,
Hamilton and Montgomery, Ayrshire in the van,
Would settle in Ireland ay' decent Scotsman.

So the Lamonts to Ulster in thousands they came,
And in Antrim and Down they became a great name,
Aye, part of the Ulster-Scots nation so braw,
They wrought hard frae Fairhead down tae Lisbellaw.

In farmin' and textiles the Lamonts made their mark,
While the old native Irish did bicker and bark,
Full five thousand moons they spilled our true blood,
Come now what may, we'll no' fear, fire or flood.

And we Ulster-Scots, no we ne'er could decide,
Where empires should rise and then fall, like the tide,
English politicking and lying, Irish bombs we ne'er fear,
For we are well planted in this domain just here.

The Enemy Within

December 2005/January 2006

Would the Jews govern their dear Israel,
With Al-Aqsa in the Knesset?
Yet we're to welcome sinn-fein-IRA,
Pontiff Tony he would bless it.

Martyrs' brigade would use their power,
To pull great Israel down,
Republicans would do the same,
In England ne'er a frown.

The Trojan horse, now don't forget,
Brought Troy down to her knees,
And in Stormont, the republicans,
Would do the same with ease.

To empower the age-old enemy,
The enemy within,
To forget our sacrifice of blood,
Would surely be a sin.

For Chamberlain and Hitler,
And appeasement tell a tale,
'Peace in our time', short-term,
You know it's bound to fail.

And our fifth column enemies,
They'll never dump the gun,
With gullible English Tony,
They're simply having fun.

So keep the gunmen where they are,
They're well beyond the pale,
And stand our ground for our wee state,
And let the 'liberals' rail.

The Hibernian Titanic

January 2006

And they've stolen the Titanic,
Every document'ry, film,
Uillean pipes and bodhrans,
Sean, Paddy, and Phelim.

'Fifteen thousand Irishmen,
They built her', we are told,
Aye, Irishmen in East Belfast,
The romantic lie is sold.

For the craftsmen they were Ulstermen,
And British to their core,
But the deeds of Sammy, Billy,
Are never to the fore.

No requiem from Lambeg drums,
Or Ulster's fluted songs,
Just misplaced cultural fascism,
To woo the movie throngs.

Complicit propaganda,
So we're side-lined yet again,
Scapegoat 'orange bullies',
That same old sad refrain.

Van Morrison's grandfather,
And Georgie Best's as well,
They worked on that great vessel,
'Not British' shinners yell.

So here it's for the record,
In case there's any doubt,
Titanic is an Ulster ship,
Propaganda? Cut it out!

Printed in the United States
108790LV00007B/344/A